I0426390

Federal Highway Administration

Climate Change – Model Language in Transportation Plans

May 13, 2010

Prepared for

Federal Highway Administration

Prepared by

ICF International
620 Folsom Street, Suite 200
San Francisco, CA 94107
415.677.7100

FHWA-HEP-11-002

Table of Contents

1. Introduction

Discussion of climate change is becoming more common in transportation planning documents. Many state DOTs and MPOs are recognizing the role that transportation policies and investments play in contributing to climate change and conversely, the potential impact of climate change on transportation systems. Long range transportation plans (LRTPs) in particular are highlighting climate change among a new generation of environmental and sustainability issues that shape transportation planning objectives.

At present, there is no federal regulatory requirement for state DOTs and MPOs to consider climate change in transportation plans. As such, agencies that are working on climate change are creating their own models for integrating climate change into their transportation plans. These models are reflected in the language that agencies use about climate change in their planning documents. Many agencies provide a robust explanation of why climate change is a transportation planning issue, context about latest developments in climate change policy, and establish new policies related to climate change.

This document provides excerpts from MPOs' and DOTs' transportation plans that discuss climate change. It is intended to guide other agencies in discussing climate change in their own plans. Although some general discussions of climate change are applicable to plans in any state or region, most of the language in existing plans is specific to the particular policy and planning context. Nonetheless, agencies that are looking for ideas about how to incorporate climate change in their transportation plans will find helpful models here.

Transportation Improvement Programs (TIPs) can also consider climate change, in a different context than transportation plans. TIPs are not policy documents, but rather lists of projects selected for funding. Any discussion of climate change occurs in the LRTP. But TIPs can incorporate climate change to the extent that climate change is a consideration in selecting projects. No MPOs or DOTs have yet explicitly incorporated climate change in their TIPs, but we offer some suggestions for how they might.

2. Model Language in State and Regional Transportation Plans

In this section, quotes from various transportation plans illustrate how agencies have incorporated climate change impacts into their plans. These can be helpful as more agencies consider how climate change will affect the transportation sector and how to include those considerations in their transportation plans. These model statements are just some examples of the variety of ways that agencies try to address the issue of climate change and transportation.

Transportation plans are unique to each planning agency. Mention of climate change and greenhouse gases can appear throughout long range transportation plans to various degrees. Generally, MPOs and DOTs address a few broad questions in discussing climate change in their plans. Text excerpts are organized according to these questions:

- What is climate change?
- How does transportation contribute to climate change?

- How does climate change affect transportation?
- Why should transportation plans address climate change?
- How does the plan address climate change?
- What existing policies and programs on climate change are relevant to the plan?
- What steps should transportation agencies take to address climate change?

2.1. What is climate change?

- "The earth's atmosphere is warmed resulting in climate change and potential adverse impacts to public health, agriculture, forests, storm frequency and intensity, mountain snow pack, smog, and rising sea levels."

  Caltrans. California Transportation Plan 2025, adopted 2006, page 21: Trends and Challenges.

- "Global climate change caused by greenhouse gases produced from fossil fuel use;"

  Caltrans. California Transportation Plan 2025, adopted 2006, page 59: Goals.

- "CO2 is a greenhouse gas (GHG) that traps heat in the atmosphere and is a significant contributor to global climate change. Some climatic changes in California have been recorded that suggest important risks lie ahead for the State's agriculture, energy, and transportation sectors."

  Caltrans. California Transportation Plan 2025, adopted 2006, page 63: Goals.

- "According to the FHWA report Integrating Climate Change into the Transportation Planning Process, there is general scientific consensus that the earth is experiencing a long-term warming trend and that human-induced increases in atmospheric greenhouse gases (GHGs) may be the predominant cause."

  Mobile MPO, Alabama. Mobile Area Transportation Study (MATS) - LRTP, adopted February 2010, page 2: Introduction.

- Climate Change definition:

  "Refers to the variation in the earth's global climate (or in regional climates) over time. It describes changes in the variability or average state of the atmosphere. Climate change may result from natural factors or processes (such as changes in ocean circulation) or from human activities that change the atmosphere's composition (such as the burning of fossil fuels or deforestation). (See also Global Warming.)"

  Puget Sound Regional Council (PSRC), Seattle, Washington. Draft Transportation 2040, adopted January 2010, page G-2: Glossary of Terms & Reference Materials.

- "Climate change is an increase in the near surface temperature of the earth most often as a result of increased Greenhouse Gases (GHGs)."

Mecklenburg-Union MPO (MUMPO), North Carolina. Draft 2035 LRTP, February 2010, page 8-9: Environment

▨ "Global climate change involves an increase in the average atmospheric temperature of the earth caused by an enhanced greenhouse effect. Changes to the atmospheric temperatures would likely cause an increase in sea levels and alter weather patterns, thereby increasing the frequency and severity of extreme weather worldwide."

Southern California Association of Governments (SCAG). 2008 RTP, adopted May 2008, page 76: Transportation Planning Challenges.

2.2. How does transportation contribute to climate change?

▨ "The transportation sector's adverse contribution to climate change is primarily through greenhouse gas emissions from cars, trucks, buses, trains and ferries."

Metropolitan Transportation Commission (MTC), San Francisco, California. Change in Motion: Transportation 2035 Plan for the San Francisco Bay Area, adopted April 2009, page 17: Overview – Change in Motion.

▨ "The consumption of fossil fuels such as gasoline, diesel and natural gas by motor vehicles has been shown by scientists to lead directly to climate change.

The challenge here is different than it is to control air pollution: carbon dioxide (along with water) is the natural end product of the clean burning of petroleum fuels, so the only way to reduce the influence of global climate is to reduce the amount of fuel burned, or to find a new fuel for vehicles that does not come from oil. Even carbon emissions from 'cleaner' sources such as natural gas, ethanol, or electricity (unless derived from solar, wind, or nuclear energy) play a role in climate change.

To reduce the negative effects of fossil fuel consumption and climate change, two themes emerge.

- First, technology changes (cleaner engines, better gas mileage and alternative fuels) have the potential to slow the effects of climate change. In addition, higher prices will regulate fuel consumption. However, there is a worry that the shift to more energy-efficient vehicles will occur too slowly to avoid potentially significant crises that will challenge the transportation system.

- This leads to the second theme: changing travel behavior. If people shift to greater use of alternative modes (transit, bicycling and walking), as discussed in Chapter 11, the effects on the environment and the reliance on oil is reduced, and people will have choices if the price of fuel rises too high."

Sacramento Area Council of Governments (SACOG), California. MTP2035, adopted March 2008, page 106-107: Environmental Sustainability.

▨ "How much can we rely on technology—clean-burning engines and fuel efficiency—to achieve objectives for air quality and global climate change, and how much on the reduction of vehicle trips?

- The only technology improvements that can be effective against climate change would have to increase fuel efficiency significantly, allow use of non-carbon fuels, or perhaps capture the carbon dioxide that goes out the exhaust pipe (an approach that offers far more promise for factory smokestacks than on-board vehicles).

How can we reduce fossil fuel consumption and slow down climate change?

- Climate change and fuel consumption are among the most vexing issues facing the region, as to where fuel conservation could be most effective and what to do to move in that direction."

Sacramento Area Council of Governments (SACOG), California. MTP2035, adopted March 2008, page 114-115: Environmental Sustainability.

"Transportation is causing global warming and other environmental degradation."

Oregon DOT. Oregon Transportation Plan, adopted September 2006, page 3: Executive Summary.

"Global Warming:
The United States is the largest energy user in the world and emits almost one-quarter of the world's greenhouse gases, primarily carbon dioxide. Greenhouse gases contribute to warming the climate. Transportation activities are estimated to be the second largest single source of greenhouse gas emissions and are responsible for 38 percent of Oregon's carbon dioxide emissions. The Oregon Department of Energy predicts that carbon dioxide emissions in the state will increase by 33 percent from 2000 to 2025 mainly because of increased driving."

Oregon DOT. Oregon Transportation Plan, adopted September 2006, page 23: Challenges, Opportunities and Vision.

"Global climate change threatens ecosystems around the planet, and our economy continues to be highly dependent on an uncertain future supply of petroleum. Solutions to both of these issues are related to reducing energy demand and finding less carbon-intense alternative fuels. While no single solution will be capable of meeting the challenges of these twin crises, a series of partial solutions implemented together can achieve sustainability. The Recentralization scenario, by reducing energy demand and CO2 emissions, can be a key part of this solution."

Delaware Valley Regional Planning Commission (DVRPC), Philadelphia, Pennsylvania. Connections: The Regional Plan for Sustainable Future, page 32: Creating a Vision for the Future.

"Transportation systems touch many complex health and environmental issues: citizen and community health, land use, natural ecosystems, species protection, and climate change."

Washington DOT. Washington Transportation Plan, 2007-2026, adopted November 2006, page 41: The Plan for the Future.

- "The transportation sector can be a positive force for improvement of the quality of the air we breathe. Investments to expand transit services, provide bike paths and other facilities to encourage bicycling and walking, and to introduce cleaner fuels and vehicles that are more fuel efficient all contribute to reducing emissions of mobile source air pollutants and greenhouse gases associated with global warming. Public education regarding the effects of auto-dependant land use and development patterns that require excessive commuting or other auto travel may also contribute to greater recognition, over time, of the connection between individual lifestyle choices and air pollution. As fuel prices reach an all time high, the need to reduce our reliance on foreign oil and turn to renewable sources and conservation measures has never been greater."

Rhode Island DOT. Transportation Plan 2030 (2008 Update), adopted August 2008, page 5-3:Recommendations

- "According to the Puget Sound Clean Air Agency, for every gallon of gasoline used, automobiles release roughly 20 pounds of carbon dioxide, one of the primary greenhouse gases contributing to climate change. In the central Puget Sound region, cars and trucks contribute more greenhouse gas emissions than any other source. Burning conventional diesel and gasoline in our motor vehicles and equipment is responsible for the bulk of our greenhouse gases and other air toxics. Choosing cleaner alternatives and retrofitting older machinery to be less-polluting are affordable ways to protect our air."

Puget Sound Regional Council (PSRC), Seattle, Washington. Draft Transportation 2040, adopted January 2010, page 40: A Sustainable Environment.

2.3. How does climate change affect transportation?

- "Climate change is expected to significantly affect the Bay Area's transportation infrastructure through sea level rise and extreme weather."

Metropolitan Transportation Commission (MTC), San Francisco, California. Change in Motion: Transportation 2035 Plan for the San Francisco Bay Area, adopted April 2009, page 14: Overview – Change in Motion.

- "Connecticut's greenhouse gas (GHG) emissions from non-renewable fuel consumption are contributing to the global climate change. The impacts of climate change on Connecticut may eventually affect our transportation infrastructure; impacts may include sea level rise, increases in the extent and frequency of coastal flooding, shoreline erosion and retreat, and increased likelihood and severity of damaging rainstorms."

Connecticut DOT. Connecticut On the Move: Strategic LRTP 2009-2035, adopted June 2009, pages 3-14: Mandates, Issues & Actions.

- "Two impacts of global warming on transportation facilities in the Pacific Northwest are rising sea levels and increased wave heights. Both could have severe impacts on Highway 101, coastal ports and other coastal transportation facilities."

Oregon DOT. Oregon Transportation Plan, adopted September 2006, page 23: Challenges, Opportunities and Vision.

- "Potential impacts of climate change upon our region's transportation system include changes in the safety, operations, and maintenance of the region's transportation infrastructure and systems. The H-GAC region is particularly vulnerable to hurricanes/tropical storms and flooding, which may be intensified by sea level rise and/or land subsidence.

  H-GAC, in coordination with the Department of Transportation and other entities are working to identify the potential impacts of climate change and variability on our region's transportation system and ultimately to develop strategies and policy options to adapt to any future changes. Due in December 2007, the U.S. Department of Transportation study "The Impacts of Climate Change and Variability on Transportation Systems and Infrastructure: Gulf Coast Study" will be particularly beneficial in assisting H-GAC's transportation and climate change planning efforts."

  Houston-Galveston Area Council (H-GAC), Texas. 2035 RTP, updated October 2007, page 49: Transportation and Climate Change.

- "In addition to reducing the impacts from the transportation sector on climate change, it is also important for the region to address the impacts from climate change. This concept is referred to as 'adaptation to climate change.' Beyond transportation, a wide variety of impacts from long term climate change may be expected in Washington state and the Puget Sound region. These include rising sea levels, increased flooding, and an increase in the frequency and severity of storms and other weather events, droughts, wildfires, impacts to water availability and quality, and impacts to crops. Specific to transportation, impacts could include the accelerated deterioration of roadways, issues related to flooding and increased stormwater, bridge damage, rail buckling, and reduced water levels in some water bodies that could affect the passage of ships and barges."

  Puget Sound Regional Council (PSRC), Seattle, Washington. Draft Transportation 2040, adopted January 2010, page 50: A Sustainable Environment.

2.4. Why should transportation plans address climate change?

- "Because the consequences of climate change are serious, the Bay Area needs to take aggressive action to reduce its transportation-related emissions, setting the example for the rest of California and for the national and international community. We will have to consider these consequences throughout our transportation and land-use planning; and we will need to ensure climate resilience in our infrastructure and development choices..."

  Metropolitan Transportation Commission (MTC), San Francisco, California. Change in Motion: Transportation 2035 Plan for the San Francisco Bay Area, adopted April 2009, page 46: Investments.

- "Our vision for the future advances the ideals of our people, our prosperity, and our planet. As we work toward achieving the region's vision, we must protect the environment, support and create vibrant, livable, and healthy communities, offer economic opportunities for all, provide safe and efficient mobility, and use our resources wisely and efficiently. Land use, economic, and transportation decisions will be integrated in a manner that supports a healthy environment, addresses global climate change, achieves social equity, and is attentive to the needs of future generations."

Puget Sound Regional Council (PSRC), Seattle, Washington. VISION 2040, adopted Spring 2008, page xi: A Vision for 2040.

- "VISION 2040 envisions a future where… Meaningful steps are taken to reduce carbon emissions and minimize the region's contribution to climate change."

Puget Sound Regional Council (PSRC), Seattle, Washington. Vision 2040, adopted Spring 2008, page 14: Regional Growth Strategy.

- "However, the automobile and suburban house will not be the only option. In a world of increasing scarcity, growing concern about climate change, intense global competition, and an aging population, provision of mixed-use, transit-oriented communities are critical for reducing CO2 emissions, attracting skilled workers, and providing for quality of life."

Delaware Valley Regional Planning Commission (DVRPC), Philadelphia, Pennsylvania. Connections: The Regional Plan for Sustainable Future, page 131: Closing the Funding Gap.

- "VISION 2040 calls for reducing our contribution to greenhouse gas emissions and preparing for the anticipated impacts of climate change. Agencies at all levels of government should seek ways to both mitigate and adapt to climate change. This includes efforts to maximize energy efficiency and increase renewable energy, reduce greenhouse gas emissions of new vehicles, reduce motor vehicle miles traveled, improve the convenience and safety of nonpolluting transportation modes such as bicycling and walking, protect the natural landscape and vegetation, and increase recycling and reduce waste."

Puget Sound Regional Council (PSRC), Seattle, Washington. Vision 2040, adopted Spring 2008, pages 40 – 41: Multicounty Planning Policies.

- "Importantly, these investments must help conserve New York State's use of non-renewable energy resources and reduce fuel emissions and greenhouse gases."

New York DOT. Strategies for a New Age: New York State's Transportation Master Plan for 2030, adopted Summer 2006, page 7: New York State's Vision for Transportation.

2.5. How does the plan address climate change?

- "Climate-Friendly Investments Dominate Spending.

The overwhelming share of plan expenditures — 97 percent — goes to support maintenance and operations, transit expansion, and bicycle and pedestrian improvements. These directly support the regional effort to respond responsibly to climate change. Many of the discrete investments in the plan are climate-friendly and aim to reduce greenhouse gas emissions from transportation sources."

Metropolitan Transportation Commission (MTC), San Francisco, California. Change in Motion: Transportation 2035 Plan for the San Francisco Bay Area, adopted April 2009, page 37: Trends and Performance.

- "To deal with the much larger issue of global warming, MaineDOT is engaged in many activities and programs, and anticipates that these efforts will need to be increased as the issue becomes more defined. Ambitious initiatives such as the Maine Climate Action Plan's goal to reduce greenhouse gas emissions to 1990 levels by 2010, and to 10% below those levels in 2020 will challenge MaineDOT's long-range delivery of transportation improvements. The transportation sector represents the largest source of greenhouse gas (GHG) emissions in Maine at about 28% of total GHG emissions. Under a business-as-usual scenario, GHG emissions will increase 48% from 1990 levels by 2020. By implementing long-range transportation actions such as slowing VMT growth, utilizing low-GHG fuel, and implementing tailpipe emission standards, GHG emissions from 2010 to 2020 can be decreased by 28.8%. Long-range strategies will need to increase the availability of low-GHG travel choices, such as transit, vanpools, walking, and biking. Complementary policies will need to address land use and location efficiency, and create transit-based incentives, to improve the attractiveness of these low-GHG travel choices."

  "MaineDOT estimates that the strategic investments in the highway and transit projects identified in his Plan will reduce emissions of CO2 by 26 to 32 thousand metric tons by 2020, and 40 to 48 metric tons by 2030."

  Maine DOT. Connecting Maine: Statewide LRTP 2008-2030, adopted December 2008, page 22: Forces Shaping the Future.

- "Transportation 2040 proposes a strategy for reducing transportation's contribution to climate change and its impact on important regional concerns such as air pollution and the health of Puget Sound."

  Puget Sound Regional Council (PSRC), Seattle, Washington. Draft Transportation 2040, adopted January 2010, page 10: Executive Summary.

- "The 2008 RTP includes programs, policies and measures to address air emissions including greenhouse gases. Measures that help mitigate air emissions, including GHG emissions, are comprised of strategies that reduce congestion, increase access to public transportation, improve air quality, and enhance coordination between land use and transportation decisions. SCAG's vision includes the introduction of a high-speed, high-performance regional transport system that may potentially reduce airport and freeway congestion and provide an alternative to the single-occupancy automobile. In order to disclose potential environmental effects of the RTP, SCAG has prepared an estimated inventory of the region's existing GHG emissions, identified mitigation measures, and compared alternatives in the PEIR. The mitigation measures seek to achieve the maximum feasible and cost-effective reductions in emissions. There are difficulties in quantifying reductions in GHG emissions due to insufficient data."

Southern California Association of Governments (SCAG). 2008 RTP, adopted May 2008, page 132: Transportation Strategy.

▪ "An issue garnering significant attention is climate change related to greenhouse gases. While there are no established Federal standards for greenhouse gases, and Outlook 2035 does not directly address the issue of climate change, Outlook 2035's overall goals for reducing vehicle emissions should have a positive effect on the Baltimore region's inventory of greenhouse-house gases."

Baltimore Metropolitan Council (BMC), Maryland. Transportation Outlook 2035, adopted November 2007, page 101: Environmental Stewardship.

▪ "In anticipation of future requirements, this RTP includes specific CO_2 reduction targets, policies and actions to reduce the need to drive and improve operations of the transportation system – two primary strategies that have been identified for the transportation sector."

Metro, Portland, Oregon. Final Draft 2035 RTP, adopted March 2010, page 1-11: Changing Times.

▪ "However, the Connections Plan also introduces several new elements to the long-range planning process, such as climate change and energy initiatives, local food production, and cultural and historic landscapes, which heighten the linkages between land use, the environment, the region's economic competitiveness, and the transportation network."

Delaware Valley Regional Planning Commission (DVRPC), Philadelphia, Pennsylvania. Connections: The Regional Plan for Sustainable Future, page 4: Introduction.

▪ "Water is of critical importance to sustain the natural environment and meet the region's growth needs. To those ends, VISION 2040 calls for maintaining and restoring the ecological functions of the region's waterways and estuaries. It calls for reducing water pollution and taking steps to address the impacts of climate change on the region's water quality and supply."

Puget Sound Regional Council (PSRC), Seattle, Washington. Vision 2040, adopted Spring 2008, page 39: Multicounty Planning Policies.

▪ "A key focus of the plan will be to protect and improve the region's environmental health. This will include ensuring that the region has healthy air that meets all standards; ensuring that transportation projects improve the handling of stormwater runoff to protect Puget Sound and other surface waters; and address emerging issues such as transportation's role in reducing greenhouse gas emissions and adapting to climate change. The plan includes a specific strategy to address state GHG goals, and vehicle miles traveled (VMT) reduction benchmarks. The four-part strategy includes Land Use, Transportation Pricing, Transportation Choices, and Technology. In addition, the Plan builds on current efforts to protect natural areas and support vibrant, livable communities."

Puget Sound Regional Council (PSRC), Seattle, Washington. Draft Transportation 2040, adopted January 2010, page 11: Executive Summary.

- "The plan is designed to keep the region's air and water healthy, sustain the region's overall ecology, assist in coordinated efforts of the Puget Sound Partnership to protect and restore the health of the region's watersheds, and lead in the development of emerging federal and state initiatives to reduce overall greenhouse gas emissions to address global climate change."

  Puget Sound Regional Council (PSRC), Seattle, Washington. Draft Transportation 2040, adopted January 2010, page 45: A Sustainable Environment.

- "VISION 2040 calls for the region to reduce its overall production of harmful elements that contribute to climate change, and commits the region to comply with state directives. An evaluation of greenhouse gas emissions and vehicle miles traveled per capita was conducted in the process to develop Transportation 2040. The results of this analysis and additional research produced a four-part greenhouse gas strategy as a central part of Transportation 2040."

  Puget Sound Regional Council (PSRC), Seattle, Washington. Draft Transportation 2040, adopted January 2010, page 47: A Sustainable Environment.

- "From the start, we extended our reach and embraced a new partnership with our sister regional agencies — the Association of Bay Area Governments, the Bay Area Air Quality Management District, and the Bay Conservation and Development Commission — to help us develop this long-range plan. With the help of our regional partners, this plan no longer focuses solely on surface transportation infrastructure but takes into account how transportation affects our land-use patterns, air quality and climate changes, and vice versa."

  Metropolitan Transportation Commission (MTC), San Francisco, California. Change in Motion: Transportation 2035 Plan for the San Francisco Bay Area, adopted April 2009, page 10-11: Overview – Change in Motion.

- "Our transportation decisions and actions can either help or hinder efforts to protect the climate, and to this end, the Commission has set aside $400 million to implement a Transportation Climate Action Campaign that focuses on individual actions, public-private partnerships, and incentives and grants for innovative climate strategies. Known for its commitment to the environment, the Bay Area is ideally suited to provide regional leadership and serve as a model for California, the nation and the world in our efforts to reduce our carbon footprint. This plan advances the fight against global warming and validates the region's reputation as a forward-looking force for change."

  Metropolitan Transportation Commission (MTC), San Francisco, California. Change in Motion: Transportation 2035 Plan for the San Francisco Bay Area, adopted April 2009, page 14: Overview – Change in Motion.

- "This plan does not include a quantitative assessment of Greenhouse Gases. However, as more consistent methods to measure GHG emissions are developed, and as legislative and regulatory mandates emerge (i.e., SAFETEA-LU reauthorization), MUMPO will address them accordingly. In the meantime, MUMPO will work on providing more education about transportation and its effects on climate change."

Mecklenburg-Union MPO (MUMPO), North Carolina. Draft 2035 LRTP, February 2010, page 8-10: Environment.

▧ "Preliminary scenarios modeling conducted in 2008 looked at how vehicle emissions might change over time with different investment choices to illustrate the region's ability to continue to meet current state and federal air quality requirements and state targets to reduce greenhouse gas emissions. None of the scenarios, including the reference scenario, achieve the state targets by 2035. The region's growing population will make it difficult to achieve the targets without other strategies. The region must identify the land use and transportation strategies needed to meet them. The region will also need to support new technology and conservation measures. The scenarios work in 2010 will evaluate a full array of land use and transportation strategies."

Metro, Portland, Oregon. Final Draft 2035 RTP, adopted March 2010, page 1-11: Changing Times.

▧ The 2035 RTP represents the first steps in H-GAC's integration of climate change into the transportation planning process. An additional step in linking transportation and climate change to the transportation planning process will be an increased recognition of the contributions of the transportation system to GHG emissions and potential strategies to reduce, mitigate and eliminate these emissions. H-GAC currently has an extensive Clean Air Initiatives program and future efforts may create linkages to other H-GAC programs and initiatives."

Houston-Galveston Area Council (H-GAC), Texas. 2035 RTP, updated October 2007, page 49: Transportation and Climate Change.

2.6. What existing policies and programs on climate change are relevant to the plan?

▧ "Furthermore, Connecticut's greenhouse gas (GHG) emissions from nonrenewable fuel consumption are contributing to the global climate change. In 2004, Connecticut became the first state to develop a comprehensive climate change action plan and immediately translate it into legislative and administrative proposals for implementation."

Connecticut DOT. LRTP for the State of Connecticut, 2004-2030, adopted July 2004, page 23: Environment, Energy Conservation & Quality of Life.

▧ "The Department is a member of the CAT and is committed to implementing transportation strategies that will help reduce fossil fueled energy and GHG emissions. The Department's Climate Action Program Report demonstrates the commitment of the Business, Transportation and Housing Agency and the Department to a transportation system that supports environmental quality. The Department's overall approach to lowering fuel consumption and CO2 from transportation is twofold: 1) making transportation systems more efficient through smart land use, operational improvements, and Intelligent Transportation

Systems; and 2) institutionalizing energy efficiency and GHG emission reduction measures into planning, project development, operations, and maintenance of State transportation facilities, fleets, buildings, and equipment."

Caltrans. California Transportation Plan 2030 Addendum, adopted 2007, page 33: Consideration of Environmental and Natural Resource Issues – Mitigation and Consultation.

▪ "In a fall 2007 telephone poll of 1,800 residents, approximately two-thirds of respondents declared that global warming is extremely important and should be one of the region's highest priorities (see pie chart at top left, page 19). Additionally, 67 percent of poll respondents said they would be willing to accept denser development in their community to maintain or improve the environment."

Metropolitan Transportation Commission (MTC), San Francisco, California. Change in Motion: Transportation 2035 Plan for the San Francisco Bay Area, adopted April 2009, page 18: Overview – Change in Motion.

▪ "Perhaps no investment recognizes the need for a multifaceted effort better than the multiagency Transportation Climate Action Campaign, which encourages behavior changes and funds innovative projects such as the Safe Routes to Schools and the Safe Routes to Transit programs."

Metropolitan Transportation Commission (MTC), San Francisco, California. Change in Motion: Transportation 2035 Plan for the San Francisco Bay Area, adopted April 2009, page 30: Trends and Performance.

▪ "The Commission has earmarked $400 million toward the Transportation Climate Action Campaign, which aims to enable individuals to develop climate-friendly behaviors, reduce the Bay Area's carbon footprint, and lay the groundwork for ongoing future climate change initiatives. The Transportation Climate Action Campaign focuses on public outreach and education efforts to alter driving and travel behaviors and to offer a suite of complementary grants, incentives, and action-oriented programs."

Metropolitan Transportation Commission (MTC), San Francisco, California. Change in Motion: Transportation 2035 Plan for the San Francisco Bay Area, adopted April 2009, page 47: Investments.

▪ "In the Commonwealth, a multi-agency implementation committee is directing the development of individual action plans for the following areas: state sustainability, state decision-making, education and outreach, energy, transportation system planning, transportation technology and operations, natural resources, and environmental management. Executive Office of Transportation (EOT) [sic] will ensure its agencies' participation and active involvement in this process. Under the Climate Protection Plan, state transportation agencies are charged with implementing a number of actions—including those highlighted below—that will aid in reducing the consumption of energy and fuel, thereby helping to reduce the emission of greenhouse gases..."

Massachusetts DOT. Commonwealth of Massachusetts LRTP, adopted 2006, page 205: Transportation and Sustainable Development.

- "To reduce GHG emissions from vehicles, the State has promulgated Greenhouse Gas Exhaust Emission Standards revising New York's existing low emission vehicles (LEV) program to adopt California's GHG emission regulations. President Obama has now endorsed these standards as a model for a federal program. This year the Obama Administration proposed rules to require passenger cars to reach a 39 mpg fuel economy standard by 2016 and 30 mpg for light trucks and sport utility vehicles. This results in an overall fuel efficiency standard of 35.5 mpg. Nationally, the transportation sector contributes nearly a third of the United States' GHG emissions. There is a need to reduce these emissions to slow the rate of climate change caused by human activity. Given the urgency and recognizing the historic next steps taken by the Administration, New York believes that a more aggressive standard and timetable can be achieved for future CAFE standards."

State of New York. 2009 State Energy Plan, adopted December 2009, page 30: Produce, Deliver, and Use Energy More Efficiently.

- "Climate change can be addressed in transportation planning with mitigation and adaption efforts. MUMPO and its partners have already employed a number of noteworthy GHG-reducing activities, several of which are described below: Fast Lanes Study; Charlotte Urban Street Design Guidelines; Connectivity Policy; Transit Planning; Congestion Mitigation & Air Quality (CMAQ) Funds."

Mecklenburg-Union MPO (MUMPO), North Carolina. Draft 2035 LRTP, February 2010, page 8-10: Environment

- "With transportation accounting for 40 percent of the region's greenhouse gas emissions, the Bay Area faces a clear imperative to address climate change in the Transportation 2035 planning process. If that by itself were not enough to motivate us, the landmark California Global Warming Solutions Act of 2006 (also known as AB 32) mandates a reduction in greenhouse gas emissions to 1990 levels by the year 2020 — effectively a 15 percent cutback from today's level. And the signing last year by Governor Schwarzenegger of Senate Bill 375 — which mandates the California Air Resources Board to work with regional agencies like MTC and the Association of Bay Area Governments to curb sprawl and reduce greenhouse gas emissions — adds momentum to this effort. This plan must take on the challenge of achieving these climate change goals."

Metropolitan Transportation Commission (MTC), San Francisco, California. Change in Motion: Transportation 2035 Plan for the San Francisco Bay Area, adopted April 2009, page 7: Overview – Change in Motion.

- "In response to the central challenge to reduce energy consumption and greenhouse gas emissions while creating more sustainable communities, VISION 2040 builds on the state Growth Management Act framework, as well as on the regional emphasis of focusing growth into centers."

Puget Sound Regional Council (PSRC), Seattle, Washington. Vision 2040, adopted Spring 2008, page 14: Regional Growth Strategy.

▣ "The CTP 2025 recognized that GHG emissions produced from fossil fuel use have direct links to the environment and global climate change. The Governor's recent "California Climate Change" initiative supports the CTP 2025 vision of sustainable transportation and improved mobility in order to mitigate climate change in California. Executive Order S-3-05, signed by the Governor on June 1, 2005, established climate change emission reduction targets for the State (shown below), and created the Climate Action Team (CAT) to coordinate the statewide effort.

The Executive Order established GHG targets to:

◆ Reduce to 2000 emission levels by 2010.

◆ Reduce to 1990 emission levels by 2020.

◆ Reduce to 80 percent below 1990 emission levels by 2050.

The Governor also signed into law Assembly Bill (AB) 32, the California Global Warming Act of 2006, giving new weight to the State's renewable energy goals. The Governor has directed State agencies to begin implementing AB 32 and issue recommendations in their CAT report."

Caltrans. California Transportation Plan 2030 Addendum, adopted 2007, page 33: Consideration of Environmental and Natural Resource Issues – Mitigation and Consultation.

▣ Prominent Laws that will shape efforts to regulate GHGs include:

◆ Assembly Bill 1493 (Pavley) - requires the California Air Resources Board (ARB) to develop and adopt regulations that achieve maximum feasible and cost-effective reduction of GHG emissions from passenger cars and light- and medium-duty trucks

◆ Assembly Bill 32: California Global Warming Solutions Act - requires reduction of statewide GHG emissions to 1990 levels by the year 2020.

◆ Senate Bill 375 (Steinberg) - requiring ARB to adopt regional GHG targets for emissions associated with the automobile and light truck sector.

Metropolitan Transportation Commission (MTC), San Francisco, California. Change in Motion: Transportation 2035 Plan for the San Francisco Bay Area, adopted April 2009, page 48: Investments.

▣ Implementation of the New Massachusetts Climate Protection Plan:

"In May 2004, Governor Romney released the Massachusetts Climate Protection Plan. The plan was the product of a coordinated effort of the OCD agencies to define actions the Commonwealth can take to reduce the emission of carbon dioxide and other heattrapping gases. These greenhouse gases form a blanket of pollution that remains in the atmosphere and may be the cause of climate instability characterized by severe weather events such as storms, droughts, floods, heat waves, and rising sea level. The plan establishes the following goals to provide benchmarks of progress and to allow necessary adjustments ensuring short-term and longterm success… Under the Climate Protection Plan, state transportation agencies are charged with implementing a number of actions—including those highlighted below—that will aid in reducing the consumption of energy and fuel, thereby helping to reduce the emission of greenhouse gases…"

Massachusetts DOT. Commonwealth of Massachusetts LRTP, adopted 2006, page 205: Transportation and Sustainable Development.

"Climate change threatens human societies and natural biodiversity because it is expected to significantly alter the ecosystems that supported the development of human civilization…Scientific evidence suggests that limiting the global average temperature increase to approximately 3.6°F (2°C) above pre-industrial temperatures may minimize the likelihood of the most severe climate impacts and is consistent with the United Nations Framework Convention on Climate Change (UNFCCC) goal of avoiding dangerous climate change. To keep warming within these limits, the UNFCCC concludes that emissions of GHGs from developed nations must be reduced by 80 to 95 percent from year 1990 levels by the year 2050. Recognizing this need, Governor Paterson issued Executive Order 24 that sets a State goal to reduce GHG emissions in New York 80 percent below 1990 levels by the year 2050. The Executive Order also establishes a Climate Action Council that is charged with preparing a draft Climate Action Plan by September 30, 2010. The Climate Action Plan will identify possible strategies for meeting the 80 by 50 goal."

State of New York. 2009 State Energy Plan, adopted December 2009, page 3 – 4: Planning Objectives.

"Further, the State Energy Plan approved by the Governor in 2002 established ambitious reduction goals for air quality emissions, greenhouse gas emissions, and energy consumption during the first quarter of the 21st century. The State's response will be comprehensive and aggressive, requiring contributions from all transportation operators. The goal is to move New York State's transportation operators to the forefront in the Nation's efforts for clean air and energy efficiency. Greater use of zero and low emission vehicles, carpooling, walking, biking and transit, commuter rail options and long distance railroad freight will contribute to a reduction of pollution. Additionally, reducing congestion is another important way to reduce emissions arising from transportation."

New York DOT. Strategies for a New Age: New York State's Transportation Master Plan for 2030, adopted Summer 2006, page 68: Environmental Sustainability.

"In 2006, the Washington State Legislature, with Governor Gregoire's endorsement, passed legislation that recognizes the importance of more stringent emission standards for new vehicles. The legislature acknowledged that:

* Motor vehicles contribute approximately 55 percent of total greenhouse gas emissions in Washington State.

* Reducing greenhouse gas emissions from transportation sources is a necessity.

In 2005 and 2006, the legislature passed bills aimed at reducing greenhouse gas emissions, including requirements for the use and production of renewable fuels. These include:

* A tax break for hybrid vehicle purchases in 2009 and 2010.

* Requirements for energy savings from consumer products not covered under national programs.

* Tax reductions for manufacturers of solar energy systems and components.

* A requirement that buildings belonging to Washington State and all buildings receiving state construction funding receive "green building" certification.

* A tax rebate for individuals and businesses that generate energy from wind, solar power, or biodigesters.

* A requirement that most diesel fuel sold in Washington State contain at least two percent biodiesel. Also, gasoline must contain at least two percent ethanol.

* A requirement that state agencies, including the Washington State Department of Transportation, increase biodiesel usage to 20 percent by June 1, 2009. This will create a better market for agricultural production of fuel oils while reducing diesel toxics and greenhouse gas emissions.

* The Energy Freedom Program will provide low interest loans for biodiesel processing and infrastructure development in order to produce sufficient quantities of biofuels in Washington State to meet the requirements and the growing demand."

Washington DOT. Washington Transportation Plan, 2007-2026, adopted November 2006, page 47: The Plan for the Future.

2.7. What steps should transportation agencies take to address climate change?

"Overarching Goal: The region will care for the natural environment by protecting and restoring natural systems, conserving habitat, improving water quality, reducing greenhouse gas emissions and air pollutants, and addressing potential climate change impacts."

Puget Sound Regional Council (PSRC), Seattle, Washington. Vision 2040, adopted Spring 2008, page 34: Multicounty Planning Policies.

"Goal: Provide a transportation system that both protects and enhances the environment, promotes energy conservation, and improves the quality of life."

Wasatch Front Regional Council (WFRC), Salt Lake City, Utah. 2030 RTP, adopted May 2007, page 6: Overview.

"Maintain and, where possible, improve air and water quality, soils, and natural systems to ensure the health and well-being of people, animals, and plants. Reduce the impacts of transportation on air and water quality, and climate change."

Puget Sound Regional Council (PSRC), Seattle, Washington. Vision 2040, adopted Spring 2008, page 35: Multicounty Planning Policies.

▦ Climate Change Goal and Policies:

"Goal: The region will reduce its overall production of harmful elements that contribute to climate change.

Policies:

- ◆ MPP-En-20: Address the central Puget Sound region's contribution to climate change by, at a minimum, committing to comply with state initiatives and directives regarding climate change and the reduction of greenhouse gases. Jurisdictions and agencies should work to include an analysis of climate change impacts when conducting an environmental review process under the State Environmental Policy Act.

- ◆ MPP-En-21: Reduce the rate of energy use per capita, both in building use and in transportation activities.

- ◆ MPP-En-23: Reduce greenhouse gases by expanding the use of conservation and alternative energy sources and by reducing vehicle miles traveled by increasing alternatives to driving alone."

Puget Sound Regional Council (PSRC), Seattle, Washington. Vision 2040, adopted Spring 2008, pages 40 – 41: Multicounty Planning Policies.

▦ Evaluate and mitigate the effects of transportation projects on the natural environment and quality of life by:

- ◆ "Continue to investigate the potential for improvements to the state's transportation system that will reduce GHG emissions."

- ◆ "Participate in multi-state and regional discussions on opportunities to divert a portion of the projected 70 percent growth in regional truck traffic to rail and barge modes in order to reduce significantly the GHG impact of freight transportation. A goal of 5 percent of truck traffic shifting to rail or barge by 2020 is desirable."

Connecticut DOT. Connecticut On the Move: Strategic LRTP 2009-2035, adopted June 2009, page 3-17: Mandates, Issues & Actions.

▦ "Implement measures to lower emissions of GHGs and air pollutants in transportation options."

Caltrans. California Transportation Plan 2025, adopted 2006, page 64: Goals.

▦ "Reduce emissions of greenhouse gases to reduce climate change,"

Oregon DOT. Oregon Transportation Plan, adopted September 2006, page 59: Goals, Policies and Strategies.

▦ "Objective 6.5 Climate Change – Reduce transportation-related greenhouse gas emissions."

Metro, Portland, Oregon. Final Draft 2035 RTP, adopted March 2010, page 2-10: Vision.

▨ Build an Energy Efficient Economy by:

"Reducing Greenhouse Gas Emissions"

Delaware Valley Regional Planning Commission (DVRPC), Philadelphia, Pennsylvania. Connections: The Regional Plan for Sustainable Future, page 70: Key Plan Principles.

▨ "To reduce greenhouse gas emissions and protect public health, the Bay Area should focus on decreasing tailpipe emissions and encourage alternatives to driving."

Metropolitan Transportation Commission (MTC), San Francisco, California. Change in Motion: Transportation 2035 Plan for the San Francisco Bay Area, adopted April 2009, page 18: Overview – Change in Motion.

▨ "Comply with the Federal Clean Air Act by recommending selected MTP2035 projects as draft transportation control measures to help reduce GHG emissions and identify transportation emission control measures."

Sacramento Area Council of Governments (SACOG), California. MTP2035, adopted March 2008, page 71: Policies and Supportive Strategies.

▨ Environment, Energy Conservation & Quality of Life Actions:

◆ "Continue to participate on the Governor's Steering Committee on Climate Change and support the Committee's efforts to implement recommendations for reducing harmful greenhouse gas (GHG) emissions generated by the State's transportation system"

◆ "Consider and address in design plans, the needs of owners of alternative fuel vehicles when constructing and renovating transportation facilities"

◆ "Encourage transportation research and projects that explore innovative solutions to GHG emissions using advanced technology, economically feasible options, and proven results for reducing emissions both in the short and long-terms"

◆ "Encourage research and projects that explore innovative solutions for responding to changing land and water patterns, including flooding and loss of coastline caused by increased frequency and severity of meteorological events which may affect components of the transportation system infrastructure"

◆ "Encourage efforts that focus on risk and response assessment, including prediction tools, products and strategies for potential maintenance, system planning, safety management and emergency preparedness issues arising from global climate change"

◆ "Encourage practices and policies that shorten delivery time and provide alternatives for goods movement through environmentally-friendly methods that reduce fuel consumption, such as coordinated intermodal transport"

◆ "Continue to implement energy performance standards for State transportation facilities, promote green building design on major capital projects, purchase environmentally preferable products, and use electronic media"

Connecticut DOT. LRTP for the State of Connecticut, 2004-2030, adopted July 2004, page 23: Environment, Energy Conservation & Quality of Life.

▪ "The air quality mitigation program includes, but is not limited to, the following types of measures:

  ◆ Encouragement of green construction techniques such as using the minimum amounts of GHG emitting construction equipment; and"

Southern California Association of Governments (SCAG). 2008 RTP, adopted May 2008, page 133: Transportation Strategy.

▪ "Goals set in the Colorado Climate Action Plan would reduce greenhouse gas emissions 20 percent below 2005 levels by 2020 and 80 percent below those levels by 2050. To meet greenhouse gas reduction goals, transportation policies need to include strategies to reduce energy consumption, dependence on foreign oil and carbon dioxide emissions from cars, trucks and air travel. Strategies may include

  ◆ Improving vehicle efficiency with technology that reduces greenhouse gas emissions in new vehicles.

  ◆ Reducing carbon-based emissions by modifying transportation systems. This could include mass transit options, measures aimed at congestion relief, and the use of more-efficient vehicles.

  ◆ Recognizing community excellence in land use and transportation and the importance of neighborhood design to limit residents' and workers' dependence on cars.

  ◆ Expanding low-carbon and no-carbon fuel options."

Colorado DOT. 2035 STP, adopted 2008, page 24: Key Issues and Emerging Trends.

▪ "Support programs and efforts that focus on minimizing fuel consumption, black carbon emissions, and single-occupancy vehicle trips, as well as addressing the environmental and health costs associated with non-renewable fuel emissions..." by the following actions:

  ◆ "Encourage transportation research and projects that explore innovative solutions to GHG emissions.

  ◆ Continue to participate on the Governor's Steering Committee on Climate Change and support the Committee's efforts to implement recommendations for reducing harmful greenhouse gas (GHG) emissions generated by the State's transportation system.

  ◆ Coordinate with northeastern states on regional strategies to incorporate GHG emissions strategies into regional transportation plans."

Connecticut DOT. Connecticut On the Move: Strategic LRTP 2009-2035, adopted June 2009, page 3-1: Mandates, Issues & Actions.

▪ "Examples of specific strategies in the Baltimore region that reduce greenhouse gas emissions from the transportation sector include truck stop electrification, park-&-ride lot improvements, rideshare coordination, incident management programs, telework promotion, alternative fuel vehicle purchases such as hybrid transit buses, and devices which allow buses to start remotely, saving idling time."

Baltimore Metropolitan Council (BMC), Maryland. Transportation Outlook 2035, adopted November 2007, page 101: Environmental Stewardship.

▨ "Make transportation decisions that conserve and optimize non-renewable resources and promote the use of renewable resources (materials, facilities, and sources of energy) and include strategies to decrease greenhouse gases and air pollutants."

Florida DOT. 2025 Florida Transportation Plan, adopted December 2005, page 14: Goals and Objectives.

▨ "The Grand Valley Metropolitan Council is working hard to stay abreast to energy changes and advancements as they relate to transportation and transportation infrastructure. As alternative fuel technology evolves our staff will continue to evaluate the applicability to plans and development projects. It is our goal to incorporate those technologies into our planning process that reduce our dependence on foreign oil as well as reduce the emission of gases that contribute to global warming, particulate matter, and chemicals that combine to form ground level ozone."

Grand Valley Metropolitan Council (GVMC), Grand Rapids, Michigan. 2035 LRTP for the Grand Rapids Metropolitan Area, adopted April 2007, page 116: Alternative Fuels.

▨ "Strategy: Implementing the State Energy Plan and Ensuring Air Quality Conformity with the State Implementation Plan…

◆ Reduction of primary energy use per unit of Gross State Product (GSP) 25 percent below 1990 levels;

◆ A 50 percent increase in the use of renewable energy as a percentage of primary energy use, so that 15 percent of energy used in the State will be from renewable sources by 2020;

◆ Reduction in greenhouse gas emissions 5 percent below 1990 levels by 2010, and 10 percent by 2020."

New York DOT. Strategies for a New Age: New York State's Transportation Master Plan for 2030, adopted Summer 2006, page 68: Environmental Sustainability.

▨ "Utilizing and maintaining existing infrastructure rather than duplicating it with new facilities could provide major economic benefits to the region. Energy consumption can be reduced by more efficient land use, such as higher density and mixed uses. This can make the region more energy independent and better prepared for energy price volatility, while lowering greenhouse gas emissions."

Delaware Valley Regional Planning Commission (DVRPC), Philadelphia, Pennsylvania. Connections: The Regional Plan for Sustainable Future, page 32: Creating a Vision for the Future.

- "The Oregon Strategy for Greenhouse Gas Reductions (2004) identifies two main strategies for reducing greenhouse gas emissions: (1) Encourage the use of hybrid, electric and other fuel-type engines instead of traditional combustion engines, and (2) guide land use choices, especially in urban areas toward higher densities, transit options, mixed-use neighborhoods and fuel-efficient designs. Additional strategies include increasing use of public transportation, freight rail, bicycling and walking."

  Oregon DOT. Oregon Transportation Plan, adopted September 2006, page 23: Challenges, Opportunities and Vision.

- "Policy: SACOG intends to use the best information available to implement strategies and projects that lead to reduced greenhouse gas (GHG) emissions:

  - Strategy: Adopt a transportation pricing policy, adopt a Safe Routes to School policy and implement a pilot program, expand public access to travel information through the 511 program, and adopt a "Complete Streets" policy.

  - Strategy: Comply with the Federal Clean Air Act by recommending selected MTP2035 projects as draft transportation control measures to help reduce GHG emissions and identify transportation emission control measures.

  - Strategy: Create an alternative fuel vehicle and infrastructure toolkit for local governments, create a public education program on individual transportation behavior and climate change, and create a regional open space strategy.

  - Strategy: Develop a regional climate change action plan, and develop and implement a construction energy conservation plan.

  - Strategy: Enhance I-PLACE[3]S model to assess greenhouse gas impacts."

  Sacramento Area Council of Governments (SACOG), California. MTP2035, adopted March 2008, page 71: Policies and Supportive Strategies.

- Goal: Employ Transportation to Sustain the Region's Vision and Values.

  "We are concerned about transportation's role in the long-term sustainability of the natural environment as it relates to ecological concerns ranging from global climate change to natural beauty. We should design local community transportation systems to enhance the quality of life of residents."

  Chicago Metropolitan Agency for Planning (CMAP), Illinois. Updated 2030 Regional Transportation Plan for Northeastern Illinois, adopted October 2008, page 24: Policy Environment.

- "VISION 2040 includes an implementation action calling for the development of a regional climate change action plan (see En-Action-7).

  Finally, VISION 2040 includes monitoring provisions in the Implementation section that call for measuring emissions of greenhouse gases and tracking local jurisdictions' programs and efforts to address climate change (En-Measure-5, En-Measure-6)."

Puget Sound Regional Council (PSRC), Seattle, Washington. Vision 2040, adopted Spring 2008, page 42: Multicounty Planning Policies.

▨ Transportation and natural environment objective.

"Promote transportation proposals that:

◆ encourage reduced energy consumption.

◆ include elements that mitigate environmental problems including offsetting carbon emissions."

Chicago Metropolitan Agency for Planning (CMAP), Illinois. Updated 2030 Regional Transportation Plan for Northeastern Illinois, adopted October 2008, page 25: Policy Environment.

▨ "In order to meet state goals and the region's broader set of desired outcomes, Metro's greenhouse gas scenario planning work will be guided by the following principles:

◆ Regional collaboration and partnerships. Addressing the climate change challenge will take a regional approach and partnerships in the public and private sectors, requiring meaningful policy and investment discussions with elected leaders, stakeholders and the public. It is only by working together and combining resources that we can hope to make real progress and be successful.

◆ Continued leadership on the integration of land use and transportation. National studies continue to show that a compact urban form coupled with expanded travel choices as key to reducing greenhouse gas emissions. Land-use and transportation policy-makers must work together to provide leadership and commit to strategies that will enhance this integration at the local, regional and state levels."

Metro, Portland, Oregon. Final Draft 2035 RTP, adopted March 2010, pages 6-26 – 6-27: Implementation.

▨ "Effective growth management and open space preservation will:

◆ Decrease dependence on the automobile for personal mobility, leading to lower levels of air pollution, less dependence on fossil fuel energy, and fewer greenhouse gas emissions.

◆ Preserve farmland and strengthen the local agricultural industry, thereby enhancing local food production at a time when rising energy prices and climate change are making long-distance food transport increasingly cost prohibitive."

Delaware Valley Regional Planning Commission (DVRPC), Philadelphia, Pennsylvania. Connections: The Regional Plan for Sustainable Future, page 38: Key Plan Principles.

▨ "En-Measure-6: Track local jurisdictions' efforts to address climate change and other environmental policies."

Puget Sound Regional Council (PSRC), Seattle, Washington. Vision 2040, adopted Spring 2008, page 101: Implementation.

▨ "Implement the principles of the Massachusetts Climate Protection Plan.

Aggressively pursue the acquisition of alternative fuel vehicles and related infrastructure for all transportation agencies.

Continue to explore the feasibility of using recycled materials for pavements."

Massachusetts DOT. Commonwealth of Massachusetts LRTP, adopted 2006, page 213: Transportation and Sustainable Development.

"Work to incorporate climate change and energy efficiency measures in the criteria for federal transportation funding."

Caltrans. California Transportation Plan 2025, adopted 2006, page 50: Goals.

"Enhance education, planning tools, and performance standards on energy efficiency, air quality, and climate implications of transportation decision-making."

Caltrans. California Transportation Plan 2025, adopted 2006, page 64: Goals.

"Continue collaborating with the California Energy Commission, California Air Resources Board, and State and Consumer Services Agency to research and develop strategies to reduce demand for petroleum fuels and emissions of GHGs, and to increase transportation energy efficiency."

Caltrans. California Transportation Plan 2025, adopted 2006, page 64: Goals.

"To combat global warming and help clean Bay Area air, the Transportation 2035 Plan:

Commits $400 million to fund a multiagency Transportation Climate Action Campaign to reduce our carbon footprint, complementing MTC's Transportation for Livable Communities Program, Regional Bicycle Program, Regional Rideshare Program, and other Transportation 2035 bicycle and pedestrian investments."

Metropolitan Transportation Commission (MTC), San Francisco, California. Change in Motion: Transportation 2035 Plan for the San Francisco Bay Area, adopted April 2009, page 46: Investments.

"MPP-DP-45: Promote cooperation and coordination among transportation providers, local governments, and developers to ensure that joint- and mixed-use developments are designed to promote and improve physical, mental, and social health and reduce the impacts of climate change on the natural and built environments."

Puget Sound Regional Council (PSRC), Seattle, Washington. Vision 2040, adopted Spring 2008, page 59: Multicounty Planning Policies.

"Consider potential impacts of global warming on transportation infrastructure and services, particularly along the coast, when designing, constructing and prioritizing investments in transportation infrastructure..."

Connecticut DOT. Connecticut On the Move: Strategic LRTP 2009-2035, adopted June 2009, pages 3-15: Mandates, Issues & Actions.

▨ "With the recent attention and emphasis placed on the areas of climate change and sustainability, and to bridge the gap into the future, the freight community needs to recognize the value of "going green." Green technologies represent a great way for shippers and carriers to become more efficient in terms of fossil fuel consumption. This will help lead to freight industry profits being less dependent on the price of crude oil. Also, creating more environmentally friendly freight movement technologies will give freight a more positive public image, which may help resolve some of the NIMBY attitudes that slow projects."

Delaware Valley Regional Planning Commission (DVRPC), Philadelphia, Pennsylvania. Connections: The Regional Plan for Sustainable Future, page 70: Key Plan Principles.

▨ Performance measure for the goal to recognize, protect and enhance the quality of the state's environmental resources and the livability of its communities through well-designed transportation projects and effective operation of the transportation system:

"Reduce Greenhouse Gas emission to 1990 levels by 2010 and to 90% of 1990 levels by 2020 consistent with New England Governors and Eastern Canadian Premiers pact."

Rhode Island DOT. Transportation Plan 2030 (2008 Update), adopted August 2008, page 5-18: Recommendations

3. Climate Change in Transportation Improvement Programs

Projects in Transportation Improvement Programs (TIPs) can be selected for their potential to help reduce transportation GHG emissions or make transportation systems more resilient to the impacts of climate change. To this extent, TIPs can also consider climate change. To our knowledge, no MPOs or DOTs have formally used GHG emissions or resilience to climate change as selection criteria for projects in TIPs.

Some MPOs are experimenting with the use of GHG emissions as a measure for evaluating projects or packages of projects in the decision-making process. San Francisco's Metropolitan Transportation Commission (MTC) used GHG emissions as a performance measure to rank and evaluate some projects in the development of its most recent LRTP. Packages of projects were also evaluated using the GHG emissions criterion. The Puget Sound Regional Council (PSRC) included GHG emissions in its evaluation of packages of projects selected in its LRTP. The use of these criteria will have a second-order effect on those projects selected for TIPs. Other agencies have considered using GHG emissions impacts as an evaluation factor for grant programs such as the Congestion Management and Air Quality Improvement (CMAQ) program.

As the use of explicit performance measures for transportation project selection expands, MPOs and DOTs will have more opportunities to incorporate climate change in the selection process for projects in TIPs. At the federal level, the new HUD-DOT-EPA Interagency Partnership for Sustainable Communities is promoting the use of performance measures in transportation decisionmaking. In California, MPOs are asked to explain the performance of their proposed TIPs relative to a specific list of performance measures.[1] Although GHG emissions are not

---

[1] California Transportation Commission, "Amendment of STIP Guidelines," October 24, 2007.

included in the list, the inclusion of some performance measure related to climate change is a logical future policy step.

For the most part, TIPs are lists of projects with little accompanying text. What text does appear in the TIP document is typically an explanation of federal and state regulations that drive the development of TIPs. Currently climate change does not factor into those regulations. Since TIPs do not develop and set policies for transportation decisionmaking, there is little room for discussion of climate change in the documents. If and when criteria related to climate change are used to specifically to select projects for TIPs, a limited discussion of climate change in the context of the criteria can be expected.

Substantive discussions of climate change are logically confined to the LRTP. The LRTP provides a venue for description of scientific and planning issues related to climate change, and development of policies related to reduction of GHG emissions and protection of the transportation system from the impacts of climate change.